Neti-Neti Meditation

Andre Halaw
Cover Photo, "House of Knowledge Variation1"
by Adrien Sifre, is licensed under CC BY-NC-ND 2.0.
Cover Design by Andre Halaw

This book is dedicated to the loving memory of Erika and Henry Sussmilch. I love and miss you, Mama and Papa.

By such sentences as "That thou art," our own Self is affirmed. Of that which is untrue and composed of the five elements, the scriptures say, "Not this, not that."
—*Avadhuta Gita* 1.25

"Form, O monks, is not-self; if form were self, then form would not lead to affliction… Feeling, O monks, is not self...Perception, O monks, is not-self...Mental formations, O monks, are not-self… Consciousness, O monks, is not-self... all those [just mentioned] must be regarded with proper wisdom, according to reality, thus: 'These are not mine, this I am not, this is not my self.'"
—*Anattalakkhana Sutta*

"There is that sphere where there is no earth, no fire nor wind; no sphere of infinity of space, of infinity of consciousness, of nothingness or even of neither-perception-nor-nonperception; there, there is neither this world nor the other world, neither moon nor sun; this sphere I call neither a coming nor a going nor a staying still, neither a dying nor a reappearance; it has no basis, no evolution and no support; this just this, is the end of suffering."
—*Udana* 8.1

Introduction

This book operates under one basic assumption: you are not your personality, thoughts, feelings, emotions, memories, body, sensations, perceptions, will, or anything else that you have come to identify yourself as, such as your gender, sexual orientation, job, your role as a parent, child, or sibling.

Most of the time we think of our inner self as a camera that leads our bodies around, our lives as personal and private experiences. For instance, when I am driving my car, no one else is present in my head sharing my experience with me. Similarly, while I am driving, I am not in the gym. I, like all other tangible objects, have a definite location—here. This, however, is a very limited view.

In reality, we are vast, empty, and attributeless, what sages call noumenon or the Absolute. Our true nature, unlike in the car and gym examples above, transcends location in space and time. It is the Nothingness that precedes, and allows for, all of being—the unmanifest basis upon which all of reality is predicated.

To borrow from the *Upanishads*, "You are That," the completely indescribable Absolute that defies all definitions and limitations. How's that for good news?

To help us make sense of this, let us imagine that reality operates on three levels. The first two compose the manifest realm (in the form of matter and other observable phenomena); the third, the unmanifest.

1. The first or *relative level* is in the realm of manifest phenomena. This conventional, everyday level of duality is where you, I, and all other things are separate. Here, a diamond is more valuable than glass and calculus is more sophisticated than finger painting. The relative level, as we shall soon see, is governed entirely by concepts.
2. The second level is manifest reality prior to conceptualization. Here, the world is one seamless whole. This is commonly called *nonduality*, *Thusness*, or *Suchness*.
3. Lastly and most fundamentally, there is the unmanifest *Absolute*. On this level, there are no phenomena whatsoever, not even in a nondual sense.

As you read the book, it is important always to remember that **the entire Neti-Neti process aims at awakening us to the Absolute. Anything short of that is simply a layover on a still longer journey. Even nondual Suchness is incomplete.**

To assign any qualities to the Absolute is to invite confusion because it transcends all concepts. In fact, it's safe to say that whatever you conceive it to be, *it isn't*, for ideas apply only to the relative level. The Absolute is completely unmanifest, which means that it cannot be seen, touched, tasted, heard, and so on.

Beyond form and even awareness, the Absolute completely evades all words and designations. *Unconditioned, deathless, formless, unborn, Nirvana, Moksha, Tao,* these are all pointers to your true nature. The same nature that all beings and all of existence shares.

Far from being a remote or esoteric principle realized only after years of intense yoga, the Absolute serves as the backdrop for all of your personal experiences and the very basis for the entire universe. It is always present; we just don't realize it because we are fixated on objects and concepts. Understood in this way, the Absolute is not separate from the world of matter. It is the fecund formlessness from which all of manifest reality originates.

In a sense, we can think of form as dense Nothingness—the manifest as the appearance of the Unmanifest.

That is your original nature.

We suffer because, like the limitless sky confusing itself with the transient clouds, we mistakenly believe that we are our thoughts, emotions, and personalities; when in fact, we are none of those things. We are trapped in the manifest realm—either on the relative, conceptual level; or if we are lucky, we might see through the conceptual haze and awaken to the nondual whole.

But who we truly are is utterly unconditioned and unmanifest.

Neti-Neti brings us back home to the Absolute by peeling away all of those layers that we ordinarily misidentify ourselves with. The process is based upon the ancient Hindu and Buddhist technique, which means, "Not this, not that." For as the 20th-century Indian sage Sri Nisargadatta Maharaj taught, "In order to discover what you *are,* you must find out what you are *not.*"

Neti-Neti trains us to look beyond our minds, bodies, gender, culture, relationships—in short, everything that we normally take ourselves to be—and recognize that none of these things is us. For this reason, this is not the kind of book that you can casually read once and then return to the bookshelf. In order to wake up, you need to internalize the process and put Neti-Neti to practice.

We are not our senses, perceptions, awareness, consciousness, emotions, bodies, thoughts. These are all brief appearances, manifestations, upon our true nature, the Unmanifest. They must all be negated and eventually transcended until only the Absolute remains.

Then we can re-embrace the world and all the aspects of ourselves that we previously negated. For when we realize that the entire universe is actually an expression of the unmanifest, we are free to dance and play as we like.

Chapter 1
The Myth of "I"

Here comes the most difficult fact for anyone to accept: there is no you. What we all mistakenly call "I" is simply just the sense of continuity created by our nervous system, along with a complex story attached to it. We assume that there is some "I" who hears and sees and smells and thinks, but actually we have it backwards.

Seeing and hearing and thinking create the *appearance* of a continuous, solid subject, which we call a person. In actuality, this "I" that we think we are is a series of mental, sensory, physical, emotional, and perceptual impressions. When we string them together, they create the sense of continuity.

But there is none.

We reinforce this sense of continuity with a fabricated narrative that we consider our personality. It is no exaggeration to say that our personal identities are the most complicated and compelling fictional characters ever. They are so convincing that we believe they are real. Talk about hoodwinked.

Actually, there is no "I." It is a mental construct that operates entirely on the relative level of reality. Its purpose is to promote survival and success; however, the "I" is also the primary source of human suffering. Ambition, greed, resentment, anger, jealousy, envy, rage, all originate from the belief in this false master called "I."

Skeptical? Good. Let's see how the "I" can withstand some critical examination.

Modern cognitive science has recently proven something that sages have known for millennia: there are thousands of gaps in our consciousness that our nervous system fills in every moment; the same way that while watching a film strip, we overlook the spaces between each frame.

If you have ever paid close attention to a poorly produced cartoon, you have witnessed how the characters skip or jump as they move, because in order to convey motion on the screen, the artists draw the sketch slightly different each time. It's really just a jittery leap between similarly drawn frames.

The same applies to our lives and who we think we are.

Reality contains way too much data for our nervous systems to process, so to scale this overstimulation down, our brains capture and digest reality in rapid-fire snapshots. This means that our lives are not actually fluid; they move in fits and bursts. Our brains and nervous systems create the *illusion* of flowing experience, when in reality they are constantly filtering out and inserting data. This mirage is called consciousness, for perception is far more interpretive and active than it is a passive reception of stimuli.

But, and here's the catch, we don't see this process at work. Instead, we think that the "reality" we experience is the way that things actually are.

Certainly, this fill-in-the gap process serves a very important biological function: it allows us to respond quickly to real, or even imagined, threats, based on inferences and deduction. For instance, if I hear a growl in the dark jungle, my mind tells me to run, it's a tiger. That inference can save my life. And certainly our sense of "I" serves social functions as well, such as prompting me to work hard and maintain a respectable reputation, and so forth. So by no means is the "I" inherently problematic, provided we see it for what it is—a conceptual construct with only relative reality.

The problem to this innate process is that we fail to see past the evolutionary advantage of *the appearance of a continuous subject* and believe that it—or "we"—is real. That's the equivalent of creating a myth like Santa Claus to keep children behaved and then beginning to believe that he truly exists.

In reality, human experience can be likened to a lightwave that can only be observed at its crest. Sensations and perceptions flash so quickly, like the peak of lightwaves, that it creates the illusion of continuity. If you have ever seen a child playing with a glow stick, swinging it in a figure eight or circular pattern, you know that *it looks like the pattern is solid and real*, yet it isn't. It's our senses and perceptual processes that turn the blurry after-image into a pattern.

The same goes for our sense of self. There is no "I"; there's simply perceptions and emotions and so on, woven together with a fabric that we conveniently call consciousness. None of them constitute a self, or what we would call an "I" or "me." In fact, the sense of what we call "I" emerges only *after our emotions or thoughts arise of their own accord.* It's a response to something that has *already* happened.

Let me explain. Our nervous system does its job of perceiving and interpreting data, followed by near instantaneous responses, *and then* the frontal cortex, the part of the brain responsible for higher-order thinking, interprets the experience in a linear fashion, *including the response that the nervous system just churned out!* This results in the experience of an "I" or doer, who is really just a story that emerges *after the fact.* The "I" is actually just misinterpreted biofeedback.

Modern cognitive science attests to the occurrence of this after-the-fact-I. For instance, when a neuroscientist stimulates a part of a test subject's brain, all of a sudden the subject remembers a childhood experience and is overcome with a flood of emotions. There was no "I" or volition involved, and yet if we asked the subject, she would wholeheartedly defend that "she" experienced the memories, instead of understanding that her sense of "I"-ness is simply yet another experience itself.

The memories occurred and *then* her brain created the experience of an "I" to rationalize the event, to frame it coherently in order to protect and guarantee her survival—one of the primary jobs of the nervous system. This is retro-rationalizing, since our "I"-ness emerges only *after* the emotion that we convince ourselves some "I" experienced.

For instance, if someone insults you, anger, resentment, or hurt might flare up without your conscious consent. Then the idea that *I have been insulted* and all of the accompanying emotions follow. This is the first time the "I" enters the storyline. Prior to this, there was no sense of "I" whatsoever; there was simply immediate experience, with no intermediary "I."

Let's look at another example: a friend told me an anecdote about a woman under hypnosis who was instructed to raise her right arm when she heard the word "marigold." Later, after she heard the trigger word and responded as told, the hypnotist asked her why she had raised her arm for what appeared to be no reason. She said that her arm was sore and that she had wanted to stretch it.

The woman completely concocted a story *after the fact,* to explain why she had raised her arm. Her mind needed an explanation, so she made one up—afterwards. This retro-rationalizing is analogous to the emergence of our "I"-sense, which manifests as the result of an emotional or mental cue, but gets falsely cast as the subject or experiencer. When in reality, the emotion or thought causes us to feel the "I"-sense, not the other way around.

If you don't believe me, observe the process yourself and you will find that most of our lives are lived "I"-lessly, for our sense of selfhood only appears when an emotion or thought summons it.

The truth is, "we" pop in and out of existence all of the time, for what we call "I" is only a fabrication as our minds weave together the stuttering mind- and sense-stream of experience and construct it into a story we conveniently call "I."

But there is no "I," not as an entity, nor as a subject or agent with volition, not even as an experiencer.

But how about awareness itself? Can't that function as a formless, surrogate "I" of sorts?

Upon first glance, awareness appears to have continuity, like a single thread that unifies all of our experiences. It functions as a kind of backdrop or screen upon which everything in our lives appears. In fact, even our sense of "I" arises inside of awareness. And while our sense of "I" comes and goes, our awareness appears fairly constant; for wherever "we" are, awareness is also present.

So maybe that's that we are, awareness…?

But even awareness has breaks, and if we pay close attention to our minds, we can spot them—brief, flickering gaps in our mindstream. Whenever our eyes leap from one object to the next, our consciousness winks out for a fraction of a second. The same occurs during thinking—there is always an empty space between thoughts.

Neti-Neti concentrates on those gaps, for therein lies our true nature—the unwavering Unconditioned.

At that level, all sense of our "I"-ness disappears, and all that can be said, in the words of Dr. Stephen Wolinsky, is, "You are Not."

Chapter 2
Negation is Transcendence

There is a longstanding debate in spiritual circles about the way to reveal ultimate reality. Some contend that reality, however we may conceive of it, eludes definitions and can only be alluded to by what it *isn't*. Others argue that, while ultimate reality or truth cannot *be captured* by words, language can point the way to it. In technical terms, these approaches are called *apophasis* and *kataphasis*, respectively.

Neti-Neti employs both.

Neti-Neti, as it appears in the Vedic and Buddhist traditions, is an analytical and meditative tool used to remind us that we—meaning our true nature, the Absolute— are "Not this, not that." We are not limited to our thoughts, emotions, bodies, desires, perceptions, and so on.

The form of Neti-Neti offered in this book is a modern, more fully developed elaboration than the one found in and employed in these ancient wisdom traditions. It is based largely on the classical Upanishadic *via negativa*, the Buddha's teaching of not-self (*anatman*), the Mahayana principle of Buddha Nature, Nagarjuna's tetralemma, and *Advaita Vedanta*'s teaching that "*Tat Tvam Asi*," the Absolute. To all of those great teachers and traditions, I owe immeasurable gratitude and thanks.

The power of this process lies in its ability to clarify what we are by revealing what *we're not*. For when we negate what we aren't, we transcend and free ourselves from it—without offering an alternative of *what we are*. In Tibetan Buddhism, this is known as a non-affirming negation. For the danger in asserting that we are anything, whether it be something as ungraspable as Awareness or Mind, is that we can easily come to define ourselves by that term.

Because ultimately we are undefinable. Anything that we can perceive or conceive of is not us, nor even ultimately real. It is conceptual, an idea, existing entirely on the relative level of reality. I'll repeat that for emphasis:

Anything that we can conceive of or perceive is a concept.

Negation is not the act of demolishing anything; it's the realization that in fact there is nothing solid to demolish at all, for anything we can perceive is only an idea.

This does not mean that the world melts into soup or that the book in your hands is completely illusory. Just as there is no identifiable "I" behind our experiences, there is no such *thing* as a book. A "book" is a designation that we automatically impute upon reality because language, culture, and history have programmed us to see the world in terms of discrete objects. What we take to be a book is actually just our nervous system's filtering of raw data and constructing them into a single convenient concept called "book."

As with the "I," the problem isn't that this innate process occurs—after all, it's biologically and evolutionarily advantageous (remember the tiger?)—it's that we don't know when it does, and therefore mistake the result, the book, as inherently real. Then people get attached to these ideas, fight to protect them, and sometimes even kill for them.

Certainly, a book has a provisional, relative reality to it. We can read it or balance our wobbly kitchen table with it. It just doesn't exist *absolutely* because it is an arbitrary construct imposed upon raw, fluid reality. To return to our three levels of reality outlined in the introduction, we can say that a book is a conceptual construct (with reality only on the first or relative level), sliced out of the raw, seamless whole (second or nondual level).

Some ideas are easier to identify as concepts. Take the number ten for example. As users of the Arabic numeric system, we have been conditioned to think of the number ten as the first double-digit number. Numbers one through nine are all single-digit and then along comes ten, and *presto!*, we are now in the double digits until 100. But there is nothing inherent in the number ten that makes it a double digit; that designation is totally arbitrary. For instance, when I count ten eggs, there's no visible leap *in reality* from single to double digits the moment that I reach the tenth egg; there's just one more egg. We could make eleven or seventeen the beginning of double digits.

Granted, we would have to redesign the interim numbers to be single digits (eleven could be "!," twelve "@," and so on), but the point is that double digits are an intellectual abstraction and do not point to anything in reality. The same applies not only to all numbers (we can never find 22 in reality, just 22 *of* something like eggs or cookies) and other abstractions such as democracy and justice, but to objects, emotions, etc.

A desk has no more reality—desk-ness—to it than the number 75 does. Both are pointing to imaginary referents.

In short, anything that we can conceive of or perceive is an arbitrary designation. For that's what our experiences are—designations (relative level) imposed upon an otherwise indivisible reality (nondual level).

What the ordinary person calls reality is actually just a complex series of overlapping and competing ideas (relative level) imposed upon the raw manifest realm (nondual). We are not only imprisoned inside of language, history, culture, gender, and grammar. So long as we fail to experience the Unmanifest, we are trapped in the first two levels because we believe that the manifest realm is "all that there is." In reality, of course, the manifest is an expression of the Unmanifest, but we do not *know* that for ourselves until we have actually penetrated the Absolute.

Neti-Neti allows us to see through all of these constructs by revealing that none of them are ultimately real; that nothing manifest has final reality, *not even the nondual level.*

This is where Neti-Neti differs from most other contemplative practices—many of them end on the nondual level, asserting that nonduality or Suchness is the Absolute. Neti-Neti disagrees. In the tradition of Nisargadatta Maharaj, it negates everything manifest, including nonduality. For anything short of the unmanifest Absolute is incomplete, an echo of a much larger and deeper reality.

What remains is the one thing that cannot be negated—the formless Unconditioned that cannot be seen, touched, heard, known, etc. After we have negated and discarded all manifestations, transcendence comes as naturally to us as laughing at the boogie man, for why be attached to or afraid of something that has no reality except as an idea?

"Not this, not that" then transforms into "beyond this, beyond that." We are not anything that we can sense, perceive, or conceive. We are beyond all of that, beyond even nonduality.

Once again, I will quote Nisargadatta Maharaj, who served as such an immense inspiration for this book. When someone asked him who or what he was, he replied, "Nothing perceivable or conceivable."

This means that, in order to realize our true nature, like Nisargadatta we must abide in and as the formless, matter-less Void beyond concepts and form—beyond the manifest realm entirely.

The process begins on the relative level by revealing that, paradoxically, there are no "things" to transcend, only concepts (level 1), and eventually proceeds to demolish even the total Whole of nonduality or Thusness (level 2). Neti-Neti rips the metaphorical carpet out from under our mental and emotional feet and refuses to offer us anything else to stand on, because ultimately there is nothing for us to rest on—not even nonduality.

There is only sheer Absolute Nothingness.

Admittedly, this practice is not for the faint-hearted, for it insists that we mercilessly abandon all of our conceptual and material pacifiers, offering ourselves nothing in their stead, nothing for us to hold onto. Not form or even nonduality. For as long as we hold onto *anything*, we are not free.

Anything we cling to owns us. This includes feelings of oneness, bliss, visions of gods and angels—it all must be negated and discarded.

In Zen, they call this stepping off of a 100-foot pole into sheer emptiness. But it's not simply nothingness. It's Nothingness, the great Void, the infinity of Non-being.

When we've negated and transcended everything, and returned to *zero*, we find what we've always had and been from the beginning—the empty, formless, attribute-less Absolute itself.

*

As we delve deeper into the process, systematically transcending body, mind, emotions, roles, beliefs, preferences, the material and spiritual worlds, we must have the courage to abandon everything. That includes our attachment to ourselves, our families, our jobs, opinions, spiritual identities, the Buddha, Jesus, Krishna,

Muhammad, God.

None of these things can help us because they are all simply ideas.

God, as most people understand and worship the term, is no different from any other idea that we have formed and mistaken for possessing genuine reality. It, too, must be seen through and relinquished.

Like with our Santa Claus analogy taught us earlier, we must not be seduced into thinking that our thoughts are real. They are merely mental maps, with no closer of a relationship to reality than a photo of water is to actual wetness. The same applies to language. As we shall soon see, there are no such things as eyes or ducks, because ultimately there are no discretely identifiable things at all.

I am not dismissing the value of thought or language. They can be very helpful while balancing your checking account or planning a vacation, as convenient shorthand for reality; but they are simply useless in helping us understand our true nature. In fact, in addition to selfishness and pride, thinking (and its attendant mapmaker, language) can be the biggest hindrance to realizing who we really are.

So the safest way to understanding the relationship between thinking and reality is to remember that **whatever you think cannot be anything more than a thought.**

*

The practice of Neti-Neti helps us to penetrate through conceptual thought in order to transcend all ideas and forms. It frees us to use our minds, rather than be used by them, for most people identify so closely with their thoughts that they completely mistake their mental maps for reality. For instance, our co-worker Larry enters the room and we might immediately think, "God, I hate him; he's so arrogant!" A strong physical response, maybe muscular tension or constrictive breathing, may accompany the thought, thus reinforcing our idea that *he really is a jerk.* After all, why would we feel this way if he weren't one?

But he's not. That's simply a label (jerk) that we have superimposed upon yet another idea (Larry). For where is "Larry"? Is he his feet, hands, eyes? Where is his Larry-ness? For that matter, how could he actually be "a jerk"? Is his hair a jerk? His teeth? How about his toes? Where is this so-called jerk-ness? In between his ears, behind his eyes?

What we've done, and we do it just as automatically as we draw the conclusion that a growl in the dark jungle means danger, is to believe *our idea* about Larry. From a holistic or nondual level, there is no more of a person called Larry than there is the number sixteen. Larry, like the idea of a jerk, has only a provisional, functional reality.

But we don't see that. We think that there really is a guy named Larry and that he is a jerk.

Because we believe this reductive caricature of Larry, we don't allow our idea of him to adapt and evolve as he does. We petrify this impression and search for reasons to affirm why he is a jerk. This leads to a lot of potential suffering, for both us and Larry.

The problem doesn't lie with thinking *per se*, but in believing our thoughts as if their content were ultimately real. Meaning is a human construction. Nondual reality— bare, manifest existence—has no meaning; it precedes and transcends it. (The attributeless Absolute, as the very predicate for the entire manifest realm, including nonduality, is beyond even form and phenomena, let alone concepts.)

Neti-Neti loosens the hold of our conceptual mind, especially our instinctive habit to believe our thoughts as if they were real and not just mental maps. It melts the rigid roles we have frozen people into, allowing us to appreciate the total unity of life, even if, from a relative point of view, people or circumstances feel unpleasant.

It's all It, even the ugly parts.

As we investigate our assumptions about the world, relentlessly saying, "This is not It. That is not It," the grip of the conceptual world begins to dissolve. As our mind stops trying to force reality into a conceptual box, reality slips back into its original nondual state, which is beyond and prior to words and concepts.

"Not this, not that" transforms into "beyond this, beyond that," as we realize that any word or idea is an imposition on seamless reality, a projection from our own minds.

This may sound confusing, but there are no jerks or flowers or lions outside of relative reality. They have absolutely no actual real-world correlates. In Buddhist terms, everything exists interdependently; nothing is separate. Thing-ness is a fiction.

Scientists say that all matter is originally stardust; I say that all forms, all distinctions, are mind stuff. For instance, every form that we see is invisibly shaped by our active interpretation of the so-called perceived "object," resulting in perceptions that mirror our mental and linguistic categories.

There are no sticks, just manifestations of the Absolute, which our minds single out from the rest of our visual field because we have been culturally and linguistically trained to call a thin, wooden appendage from a tree a "stick." There are no dogs, just the Absolute manifesting as animals that we label "dogs." No water, just… You get the picture.

Neti-Neti exposes everything we can conceive of to be just ideas, thus negating their reality as things. And I mean everything.

For instance, if we ask, "What is this emotion I call anger? What does it feel like? Where is its anger-ness?" When we find no selfhood or solid substance to it, the emotion swells to fill our entire being. Anger returns to its true nature as simply another expression of nondual reality, seamlessly interwoven into the very fabric of our experience.

Not as an object in our awareness, but *as* our awareness itself.

Now granted, even at this point "anger" may still not feel like how we want or expect life to feel—like the joy we experience when we are reunited with a loved one or our excitement at receiving a well deserved job promotion—but it loses its definitiveness and its power as a "negative" or "unpleasant" emotion. As does pain, fear, depression, or any other emotion, sensation, or thought.

We begin to transcend them, for as they lose their definitions and boundaries, they also lose their power to define us and the world.

The *base object* (anything that we can sense, hear, smell, taste, touch, and so on) of our investigation dissipates into non-sense, which I literally mean *to lack sense or logic*, and all that we are left with is a nondual experience beyond words—what Buddhists call Thusness or Suchness. Words cannot express nonduality, not because it is esoteric or mystical, but because *direct* manifest reality transcends words and concepts; it precedes human logic.

This experience of nonduality is what some Zen masters call "Don't-know mind" because we are no longer governed by the false reality of thoughts. The conceptual overlay, which normally obscures immediate manifest reality from us, drops away.

"What is this, truly what is it? Is it me?"

"Not this, not that," the great Indian sages taught us, for none of these things we identify with (or resist, for that matter) are us. We cannot be contained by anything within the manifest real, *not even the nondual totality*.

We are the Absolute, yet the way we normally understand and experience the world is as ideas.

We live in an illusory world of concepts without even knowing it, trapped inside of a fortress of ideas built upon more ideas. Most of the time we don't eat food; we eat our ideas of what the food is, or more to the point, what it *should be or taste like*. For instance, when we eat a slice of pizza, rather than taste it, we might be preoccupied with comparing it to what we think is better or worse pizza. In this sense, we aren't eating *this* slice of pizza as much as we are eating how we think it should taste, or even how we think other pizzas taste in relation to this one.

Too often, we don't interact with people; we interact with our ideas of who they are or think they should be. We see them as jerks or heroes or failures, rather than understanding that who and what they are defies all conceptual categorization, that ultimately they are the infinite Absolute just as much as we are. This misidentification leads to confusion and suffering, both for ourselves and others.

We don't live authentically. Self-consciously, we live out the ideas of who we think we are, were, will or should be. Lives of quiet desperation, as Thoreau wrote.

We worry about succeeding or failing, as if our performance on some exam or evaluation report could ever affect who we truly are as the stainless Unconditioned. But we worry ourselves into knots, doubting and internalizing all of these stories as if they were real, rather than seeing them for what they are—more thoughts with no actual correlates in reality—in the same way as we mistake our sense of "I"-ness as being anything more than the conceptual representation that it truly is.

Neti-Neti is the sword of wisdom that cuts through delusion, revealing the true reality that is never hidden, that is always right in front of us, in us, and *is* us. The reality that precedes both conceptualization *and* form.

All we need to do is see past our attachment to thinking and the entire manifest realm, to simply trust that we, as expressions of the Absolute, are "not this, not that."

Chapter 3
Negation in Action

In our daily lives, we constantly confront things, events, and people that we deem unpleasant. Our emotions surge from joy and elation to frustration and anger like the ocean tide. We spend much of our time chasing after so-called pleasant emotions and states, and running from or pushing away painful ones.

In Hinduism and Buddhism, this is *Samsara,* the vicious cycle of unhappiness, suffering, and frustration that marks most of our lives most of the time. Up and down we go in fitful bursts from satisfaction and even genuine happiness to downright misery—and sometimes over the course of only a few hours—all because we are at the mercy of our temperamental thoughts and emotions.

Fortunately, there is an alternative, a saner way to live. No, it does not entail controlling our minds through positive thinking or changing its contents at all. Exchanging one thought for another is not the solution; for all thoughts are impermanent and insubstantial, and thus lead to suffering if we identify with or attach to them.

The solution rests in simply recognizing that our thoughts, emotions, bodies, etc., are not us or even ours at all. We are beyond all of them. To restate: **we are not our minds, emotions, bodies, or perceptions; we transcend all of them. We are not even the awareness in which they all arise. We are the Absolute, from which everything, including our sense of "I," springs forth.**

So why worry about something that is not us, ours, and cannot touch who or what we truly are? Something that is not a "thing" at all?

The key to freedom lies within that very simple recognition that, *I am not this, I am not that. I am beyond all of it.*

This is the profound wisdom of Neti-Neti.

This chapter outlines the investigative process to use in everyday life, or "in action" as I like to call it. It serves as both a warmup to prepare you for the main practice, detailed in the next chapter, as well as a summary of how to enact Neti-Neti throughout your daily life.

First:

1. Identify the *base object* (again, the base object refers to anything that we can perceive, sense, experience, or investigate). For instance, it might be a troubling emotion or thought, a physical sensation, or even a perception. For the sake of convenience, let's concentrate on a strong, common emotion like frustration as an example.

Instead of inquiring into its origins—why we feel frustrated, and especially *the story surrounding the emotion*—we must first distance ourselves from it in order to defuse its emotional power.

Take a deep breath and try just to witness it. Settle into your pure, unsullied capacity to witness events or states as they pass by.

Most of the time we are so enthralled by the emotion, event, or thought, that we fuse with it. Not only is there no "I" in this state—which is not necessarily problematic—but there is no self-awareness. There is simply anger or anxiety or happiness.

It's important to acknowledge that merging with our experience is helpful in some contexts. In Zen Buddhism, for instance, closing the gap between awareness and objects is often viewed as the pinnacle of practice. When a basketball player is about to shoot a three-pointer, any gap between her and the shot can lead to failure, for the intellect simply acts as an impediment in such circumstances. The same goes for a concert pianist or jazz saxophonist. Spontaneity and fusion are desirable, if not downright necessary, for success in these contexts.

So "flow," as these experiences are known, can serve a useful purpose (see the work of Mihaly Csikszentmihalyi). These optimal states of performance, while often beneficial, must be transcended like all experiences, nondual or otherwise.

The Absolute is completely unmanifest. Anything short of the Unconditioned is just a rest stop.

Back to our example of frustration: identifying or merging with our emotions often leads to delusive action. After all, who is more likely to act unskillfully than someone consumed with anger? Not to mention, why merge with "frustration" if there is no such thing as frustration, let alone no "I" to be frustrated in the first place?

2. Experience it. Next, experience the object as fully as possible. This approach is stressed in most forms of awareness meditation such as Insight Meditation (*vipassana*) and *zazen*. Investigate the sensation, in this case, frustration. What does it feel like? What's its texture? Where does it manifest or elicit a physical reaction—in your chest, hands, stomach, eyes?

What's vital to note at this stage of meditation is your response to the *base object*. How do we compound frustration with resistance, judgment, guilt, or self-righteousness? Where do these manifest in your body?

Notice all of these as they appear.

Be particularly mindful of when you are witnessing an emotion in the hopes of making it disappear. This is a very subtle expectation that creeps into meditation. We secretly want the emotion or physical sensation to vanish, especially when we consider it painful or unpleasant. Resistance only makes the *base object* feel more real, more solid, when it is actually just a label we have superimposed on our field of experience. Your intention at this point should be simply to *experience it fully*. Don't try to change anything. When you catch yourself trying to tamper or vanquish the *base object*, take a mental step back.

View it, don't push it away or pursue it. If the object disappears under scrutiny because it is so impermanent that it cannot persist, then it has self-negated. We can then ask, "Where has it gone?"

All phenomena arise from and subside into Emptiness, the primordial void of the Absolute. "What was it, anyway?" we can then ask. Just as silly as we feel after awakening from a nightmare, as the dream and its imaginary threat quickly fades, the reality of the object *as anything more than an idea* becomes equally absurd.

The more skilled you get at distancing yourself from your emotions and thoughts, the more layers you will note in any given emotional, mental, or physical event—the more texture you will notice in your daily experiences.

This is a recognition of the *base object,* as well as all of the other extra baggage that we add to it.

Most forms of awareness meditation instruct us to continue investigating the object until it dissipates, in order to demonstrate its impermanence and break our attachment to it. Dissolution, you will find, occurs very quickly after you become aware of the *base object.* For instance, anger tends to cool once we notice it; fear or anxiety often fade. That's the power of awareness in action.

But awareness alone is not our goal.

3. Discern labels. Now that you are familiar with the *base object*—its place of concentration, texture, and feeling—observe the labels that you attach to it. For instance, we might think that frustration is *justified* or *wrong*, or maybe even *empowering.* Some meditation traditions encourage students to label their thoughts in order to dis-identify from them. For instance, a student might silently note, *Jealousy has arisen again.* Then later, *Oh look, another thought about me desiring the attention of others.*

Neti-Neti, on the other hand, recognizes that labels are already there. Without even knowing it, we immediately label emotions all of the time: *good, bad, righteous, unnecessary*, etc. There is no need to add more labels. In fact, that's why we grow attached to or flinch from objects: because we are seduced into thinking that they are inherently good or bad, when they're not. To quote Hamlet, "There is nothing either good or bad, but thinking makes it so." So why add more labels to an already sticky mess?

In Neti-Neti, we see through our thoughts in order to transcend them, so refrain from adding any further layers of conceptualization.

Our task at this point is simply to *witness* our reflexive labeling process. To return to our example about frustration, we might recognize several layers surrounding what we ordinarily regard as a simple emotion. There's the emotion, coupled with a physical response and some sort of nuanced thought, as well as the secondary labels we apply, like shame or even further frustration in response to our initial frustration.

4. Delabel. Watch the labels and allow them to fall away.

A fundamental tenet of most forms of meditation is that we must be aware of something—a habit, assumption, impulse—before we can free ourselves from it. To apply this to this stage of the negation process, we now spot any assumptions or labels we have about a *base object* in order to defuse them.

For instance, if we observe that fear emerges in response to our frustration—perhaps because we are afraid of what our frustration might drive us to do—we not only arrest the fear from growing stronger, but we gain freedom from it through the distance that objective awareness grants us. For the longer we observe an emotion or thought without actively engaging it or acting upon it, the more detached we grow, as it becomes apparent that *whatever we are observing is not us*, and thus we are free from it. We need not be enticed or distressed by objects that clearly are not us or ours.

Hence, the labels of *good* and *bad* lose their potency and eventually dissolve, as we recognize that they are simply mental projections that are complicating the *base object* of our investigation.

Delabeling is integral to negating and transcending the object, for in order for us to transcend a label, we must first identify it. Otherwise, unstated beliefs remain hidden and therefore continue to operate beneath our awareness.

5. Empty it. The next stage only emerges when we have successfully dropped all labels and concepts about the object. To borrow from a Zen expression, when we stop picking and choosing, labeling some experiences as good and others as bad, then we are finally free to experience the object, and thus life, free from conceptual overlays.

At this point, the *base object* ceases to be an object. When the conceptual categories fall away, its distinction as a discrete emotion or perceptual object begins to shimmer, so to speak. Its former concrete identity gets cloudy and just...*Is*.

This is a taste of Thusness or nonduality, what Buddhists call emptiness (*sunyata*). For it is only when we have seen *through* the conceptual veil (or labels) that we have constructed about an object, that we are free to experience it fully. Paradoxically, there no longer is any "thing" for us to experience because we realize that **the thing *was* the label**.

This is the beginning of transcendence. Experiencing nonduality is the first step towards realizing the Absolute.

We now realize that what we previously called "frustration" was actually just an idea, a false imputation of boundaries and selfhood (in this case frustration-*ness*) on the inexplicable and uncategorizable Thusness. This is why in Neti-Neti we avoid labeling the object because *the object itself is a label, a thought.*

This and the previous step, the **delabeling** stage, are the most difficult to complete, so don't get discouraged if nothing radical happens. What we are literally doing is systematically deconstructing the mental highways we have paved over the course of our entire lives.

It takes time.

6. Transcend duality. Now we ask, "What is this? Is this me? Is there any "I" in there?" It's interesting to note that traditional forms of Neti-Neti leap past all of the previous steps, as well as this one, and instead simply insist that you are "Not this, not that."

However, I believe that it is absolutely necessary to see through the labels we have attached to objects in order to fully free ourselves from the subtle ideas that accompany them. This is one fundamental way that Neti-Neti Meditation differs from the traditional form.

We cannot simply be content with rejecting objects as not ourselves, for concepts can still retain a subtle hold over us. Another way of saying that is: we will continue to grasp at objects *until we realize that they are empty of every quality we falsely imbue them with.* It's not enough to say that my body is "not me," because that still assumes that there is a "thing" to call a body, not to mention an "I." As long as we continue to believe that "bodies" exist, that the term has any discrete reality, we will continue to grasp at "bodies," no matter how many times we negate them.

The Buddha addresses this at length in the *Diamond Sutra.* He says that even though we call them "bodies," in reality there are no things to which the word "bodies" refers. The same applies to people, countries, and selves. As the sutra teaches, the only way to be truly free of objects is to *empty* them of their supposed self-hood, which means to demonstrate that there is no locatable *body*-ness to a body, no *eye*-ness to an eye, no *evil*-ness to evil. This negates their supposed selfhood, revealing that a body is only an idea, and hence is no-*thing* to attach to.

After we have seen through to the complete and utter emptiness of an object—empty of all the thoughts and labels we impute upon it—its supposed separation from everything else in the universe vanishes. When we experience this non-separation, we are ready to penetrate into, "What is *this*? Is *this* me??"

Not until then.

As you have probably already guessed, the answer to all of these inquiries is a resounding "no," for the simple fact that there is no-*thing* called "I" ever to be found in our experience. Yet, even that falls short of the truth, for saying "no" still implies that there are actual "things" that can be separate from one another, including the ultimate phantom itself, "I." Instead, like one of those drawings that appear to be a duck from one angle and a rabbit from another, we are left with the paradoxical feeling that we are simultaneously connected to and yet somehow beyond the experience.

It's not coincidental that the *Heart Sutra*, the seminal Mahayana Buddhist scripture, ends with the mantra, "Gone, gone, gone way *beyond*!" For we are "beyond" any verbal expression, beyond even nonduality.

Alternately, we might inquire, "Who is experiencing this?"

As you can see, our scrutiny is now turning away from the object and inward to the supposed "I" or subject experiencing the object, sensation, or perception; to the imagined witness separate from what is seen, as a subject or agent capable of volition and action upon an "outside" world.

Where is this "I"? Where does it reside? Who am I?

If you want to condense those three questions into one, ask, *"Who is the one experiencing this?"* This is the central question in Sri Ramana Maharshi's *atma vichara* or Self-enquiry—"Who am I?"

Where is this "I" that we assume exists? It is nowhere to be found. It's a boogeyman, a phantom whose imaginary presence is often felt but whose identity is never truly revealed. It, like all other "things," is merely another idea. And as I have stressed earlier, ideas have no actual correlates or substance.

Words cannot describe the experience of subject and object collapsing. The best I can do to convey it is to clap my hands together. *Wham!* Not like the massive demolition of a building, because there was never any building in the first place. It's more like the moment you recognize an old friend's face.

Aha!

During your daily routine, you may feel satisfied practicing steps 1 – 6. That's perfectly fine. For most people, living nondually is ideal, functioning with as much grace as poise in your everyday life as Michael Jordan did on the basketball court.

However, you may want to proceed further, especially if you have developed a strong enough Neti-Neti practice to have experienced the Absolute. I provide step 7 for those of you who, in addition to having awakened to the Unmanifest through formal meditation practice (see next chapter), would like to integrate an awareness of the Absolute into their everyday lives.

7. Negate all that remains. The final step in the process is to negate awareness, its contents, and the entire world. Our true nature, the formless basis of the whole manifest realm, cannot be sensed, perceived, known, or experienced in any way. Therefore, anything that we can see, hear, smell, and so forth, is not the Absolute (in its purest form), and must be negated.

Anything that you are currently experiencing—the entire panorama of sights, sounds, thoughts, etc.—must be penetrated and cast aside. Even nondual experience needs to be abandoned, for it is not the final or ultimate truth. The void of Thusness (second level) is still not the Void of Nothingness (third level or Absolute).

Think of it this way: all experiences change, the Absolute does not. The way to isolate the unconditioned is to discard the conditioned.

Become aware of everything in your field of experience and say, "All of this is impermanent. None of this is final." It is all Neti-Neti.

Everything in the world comes and goes. Negate it. Realize that none of it is ultimately real. Whatever you hear is not It. Whatever you see is not It. Whatever you feel is not It.

Continue through your entire current experience and negate everything present. None of it is It.

But there is one thing that is real and cannot be negated. What is that? When we have emptied the entire world of its contents, including consciousness, what remains?

Ask yourself, "What is the one thing that is not subject to change at all?"

That is the Absolute. That is your true face. It has no form, shape, volition, intelligence, sentience. No anything, which is why I call it the great Nothingness.

*

At this point, there are no longer any things to say, "Not this, not that" about, for their assumed identities have been revealed to be merely conceptual. There is not even any more consciousness or awareness—that too has been negated. So what remains?

The process of negation has negated itself, for without anything to investigate or anyone to do the investigating, the process becomes meaningless.

And so we have transcended the process itself. It is nothing special, and yet everything changes. The world becomes less edgy as our sense of self and separation diminishes, and eventually drops away altogether.

A flow chart of the Neti-Neti process in action might look something like this:

Supposed object → Collapses as labels are removed →

Supposed subject → Collapses as subject's identity is revealed to be

nonsensical =

nonduality as all objects meld into awareness →

negation of all that remains, including consciousness = the Absolute

If this sounds complicated, here is a summary:

1. Identify the object. Like a skilled archer, zero in on the emotion, thought, or percept.

2. Experience it fully. Stabilize your mind and body with the breath, then concentrate on the object. Do not, however, fuse with it. Keep a safe distance while you witness it. Avoid flinching from or pursuing the object, as is our normal tendency. Let the object wash away.

3. Discern the labels. As you investigate the object further, observe the stories, judgments, and evaluations you have assembled around the object. This may be very difficult, but resist subscribing to the labels. Ordinarily we just assume that they are true, but here we are simply examining them like a scientist studying specimen under a microscope.

4. Delabel it. Allow the labels to fall away. They have no reality whatsoever, so if we simply *see* them, we will soon see *through* them. Realize that they are not inherently good or bad; it's thinking that creates these dualities and the inevitable suffering that follows.

5. Empty it. Like in one of those Magic Eye paintings in a shopping mall, where you have to relax your eyes in order to recognize the image inside of what appears to be just a haze of colors, allow your mind to slip back into its original state. Except unlike in the Magic Eye where the hidden image pops *out* of the landscape, at this stage in the process you allow the pattern—the object and its distinctiveness—to recede, blend *back into* the primal nondual landscape. *Just* see, *just* hear, *just* taste, *just* touch, without adding anything to the process. This is the midwife to nonduality.

6. Transcend duality. Now that the object has been emptied or negated, ask, "Who is seeing this?" Penetrate into the core of non-separation by inquiring into the supposed subject. Where is this "I"? Just as the object of our perceptions has been reduced to absurdity, so too is the imagined subject. When both are negated or emptied of separate identities, then there is no longer anything (or things) to say, "Not this, not that" about, including any "I" to do the saying. There is simply Thusness.

7. Negate all that remains (optional). Anything that you experiencing is not It, so abandon it all. None of it is ultimately real; it is all Neti-Neti. Ask yourself, what is the one thing that cannot be negated? The answer, of course, is the Absolute, but don't be satisfied with a verbal answer, *become the* answer.

Negate and discard everything that you sense and perceive. None of it is the Absolute. Return to Nothingness.

At this point, the Neti-Neti process has successfully deconstructed, negated, and transcended itself.

We can use the Neti-Neti process at any time during our daily lives: as we wait to board an airplane, ride in a taxi, experience nervousness before a job interview, or exercise at the gym. Once you have thoroughly investigated the object, keep asking yourself, "Who is the one experiencing this?" You are not looking for a verbal answer, or even seeking some object you can *know* with your mind, for your true nature can never be reduced to an idea or object. After all, anything that you can perceive or conceive of is an idea, not It.

The answer cannot be found in words. The question can only be "solved" by penetrating into the empty, limitless space of nondual awareness, where there is no separation between mind and its contents or awareness and it objects. Then abandon that too. No words can enter there, not "Neti-Neti" or even "beyond."

That is transcendence found right here in this world, in this body, in this life.

Chapter 4
Neti-Neti on the Cushion

We just examined how to use the Neti-Neti process during our daily routine. For instance, while we are gripped by anger when someone says something rude to us. The entire process can take anywhere from several seconds to minutes, depending on how much time and physical space we have to explore the emotion, its strength, and duration.

The goal is to gain clarity about the emotion, to recognize what it is and *isn't*. It is not a thing (level 1), or something to be feared or repressed. It is also not us, our identity, nor an aspect of the two. At the same time, it, like all phenomena, has no separate reality from the rest of manifest reality.

But that's not where the journey ends; nonduality (level 2) is only 75% of the way there. We must still transcend nondual Thusness and penetrate to the formless noumenon. When we have a stable insight into the Absolute, we realize that the entire manifest realm is actually an expression of the Unmanifest. Then there is nothing to perform Neti-Neti on. That is full negation.

Chapter 3 serves as a kind of warm up for the main event. In this chapter, we will explore how to integrate Neti-Neti into formal meditation practice.

The process outlined in the previous chapter is most effective when we have a solid daily meditation practice. I chose to include it first since we can engage that aspect of Neti-Neti on-the-go, and while the process might appear complicated, it occurs very quickly, sometimes in a matter of seconds. Realistically, most people, at least in the beginning stages of practicing Neti-Neti, will only be able to navigate up to step 6, **Transcend duality.** This is perfectly understandable. In order to penetrate to the deepest level of reality, we will have to develop a strong meditation practice first.

If you are interested in realizing the Truth, your true nature, the Absolute, then this current facet of practice, concentrated meditation, is crucial. This chapter details the heart of Neti-Neti, and is indispensable in developing the skill and mental balance that we will need to make the previous chapter's practice successful, as well as any insight into the Absolute possible.

Like any other form of meditation, you should find a relaxing spot where you will not be distracted by obligations or commitments. Yet, unlike in other meditations where you keep your eyes half-open, after several minutes and you have stabilized yourself, I recommend that you close your eyes. I find that it is easier to concentrate with my eyes closed.

After you have practiced the following process several times, you may decide that the order I have presented the steps in does not work best for you. I have a student who said that negating the body (the first step below) is the most challenging for him. I suggested that he move that stage to the end of his meditation session, and to spend more time negating the body. So by all means, feel free to engage the process in whatever order suits your needs and feels the most natural to you.

Now:

Get settled. Sit upright in a chair or on a meditation cushion. Find a comfortable position and place your hands on your lap or knees.

Follow the breath. Allow your breathing to slow. Our breath keeps us alive and yet we pay so little attention to it. Study the course of the breath, as it enters your nostrils, fills your lungs, expands your abdomen, nourishes your body, and eventually exits your nose. Relax.

Close your eyes and settle into the darkness. Continue this for several minutes, until you feel comfortable in the infinite black expanse.

Posture and form

Examine your body. Allow your body to do what it does—breathe, swallow, and adjust its position. Without appealing to your imagination or memory, ask yourself, "Where does this body begin and end? What *is* this body?" Since you can't feel all of the body's boundaries while sitting motionless, how do you know for sure where your body ends, or even *what* your body is unless you rely on your memory?

Where is your body? *What* is it? That may sound silly, but the more frequently and deeper we inquire into the nature of things that we take for granted as facts, the less substantial they feel, and the more conceptual they are revealed to be. As we will see throughout this chapter, the body is ultimately nothing more than an abstraction that we impute substantial reality onto.

If there is any tension or discomfort in an area of your body, enter it. Concentrate on the region, observing the texture and nature of the discomfort. As in the previous chapter, investigate any labels or stories you have constructed around the sensation, such as, *Why me? Why am I the one who has to…?*

Then let the label return to the emptiness from which it emerged. The label is just another idea for you to relinquish.

Where is the "I" in the body? Inquire into the supposed location of the self in the body. Where does it reside? Ask, "Where am *I*?" Most people regard the head as the seat of their being, so we will start in the exact *opposite* end of the body and work our way up.

Focus your attention on your feet. Ask yourself, "Am I my toes?" Wiggle them to thoroughly engage and answer the question.

Of course the answer is *no*; we cannot be our toes. How would we drive or talk if our toes composed the entirety of our being? No individual part of our body is "I." They are all Neti-Neti, not this, not that, for ultimately we are beyond the body and the entire realm of form.

Even more radically, the more we investigate our toes for any "toe-ness" the more inane the idea of "toes" becomes. Like repeating a word over and over again until it becomes unintelligible, the more that we inquire into "toes" the less sense that "toes" makes because "toes" is a concept with no final reality to it. Certainly, on a day-to-day basis, we use and must acknowledge its provisional reality, but "toes" have no *absolute* counterpart in reality.

Now move to your ankles and repeat the self-inquiry. You may not need to continue the process for the entire body depending on your own personal psychological makeup; you might move from your knees directly to your head.

For some reason, probably because our heads contain so many sensory organs, we

33

identify our-*selves* very strongly with our heads. (For now, we are examining just our heads, not the sense organs. That is coming soon.) Perhaps we can attribute it to our science-oriented culture's emphasis on psychology and neuroscience, but for some reason we have an intuitive sense that our "I"-ness resides in our skulls, behind our eyes. Even though it doesn't, we cannot shake that intuitive feeling. That is why it is so important to dig deeply into the unstated assumption that some self abides or exists inside of our head. It doesn't because the "I" is a myth.

Inquire, *Where is this "I" in my head?*

But our head is also "Not this, not that" because "head," like "toes" and "hands" and "I," is just another idea. What we are transcends all of our body parts.

Is my body as a whole "me"? Just as we systematically negated all of our individual body parts as potential residences of the "I," now we move our attention to the entire body, the total assemblage of all our organs and limbs. Despite the logical conclusion that we are not any individual part of our body, we probably still have the nagging feeling that we *are our body* or that the "I" resides *in* our body. Or perhaps that I own or possess my body. Which is why this stage is so important to follow the previous one.

Ask: *Where is this "I"? How can the body be the "I"? If I am the entirety of the body, then where would "I" go if I lost a limb?*

Remember, these are not mere intellectual or philosophical questions. Ask them with every ounce of energy that you can muster, for the wisdom and freedom they offer is beyond measure. Effectively, we are demolishing the shackles of attachment and delusion, and liberating ourselves to return to the great reality of the Absolute, which is our and all beings' true nature. For just as with our individual parts, our bodies are not "I," "me," or mine because ultimately there are no bodies. "Bodies" is yet another arbitrarily drawn concept.

And as before, they are Neti-Neti. Our true nature is beyond the concept of "body."

Senses

Are my sense perceptions "me"? To immediately follow our investigation of the body, we will move through our perceptions.

Ask yourself, *if I were to lose my sense of taste, would I still exist? Granted, I might not be the* exact *same, but would I still be "me"?*

You are not your tongue or its ability to taste, for your true self is beyond any sensory organ or its sensory experience. Proceed to the nose, the ears, and then make your way to your eyes, which are the most complex of all of our sense organs.

Open your eyes and ask, *Am "I" my eyes or what they see? Are they "I," "me," or mine? If I went blind, would I still be me?*

Of all their senses, humans identify most intimately with their eyes. We are such visual creatures that very often we take for granted how much of our identity we invest in our eyesight.

That is why it is so critical to thoroughly transcend any assumption that you are your eyes, your vision, the owner of them, or that "eyes" are anything more than an idea. Keep investigating. Ask yourself, *Where are my eyes?* What *are my eyes?*

Nowhere can we find a concrete answer. The deeper we search for our "eyes," the more absurd the idea of "eyes" appears, for that is all that "eyes" are—an idea. If eyes had any kind of irreducible, ultimate reality, then they could produce sight all on their own, without the aid of light or an object. But they can't; for they, like all other organs, rely upon the complex labyrinth of the human nervous system to function. This means that they are not independent, and any reference to "eyes" is simply an arbitrary designation, a concept.

So we then ask, *When I close my eyes, where do "I" go? If I were my eyes, where would I go every time I blink? Am I my eyes?*

Now, the self, like our "eyes," degenerates into absurdity. All we can say is, Neti-Neti.

The sense of self, however, is very cunning, and soon the question evolves into whether we are the *process of perception.* So ask, *Is this act of "seeing" me?*

The human mind is very crafty; it creates phantasms where none exist. If we cannot find a self, then our shrewd imagination may just project one onto the very process of perception, regardless of whether it is seen as occurring inside or outside of our body. For instance, most of the time we imagine that our perception works something like this: S < O, where S equals the subject, us; the < equals our seeing or hearing; and O represents the object. At this stage in Neti-Neti, after we have negated the organs and even the external perceptions, we might impute selfhood to the *process* of perception itself, <, especially since it has a kind of formless quality. How seductive.

But simply close your eyes again and ask yourself, *Where did my seeing go? If "I" am "seeing" itself, where did I just go?* Obviously, if seeing ceases and yet our consciousness persists, we are not the act of "seeing" either. Thus it is not "I," "me," or mine, for we transcend them.

Continue the process for all of your other senses: feeling, hearing, tasting, and smelling. They are all Neti-Neti, "Not this, not that," or from a Buddhist perspective, they are not-self. When we investigate them as deeply as possible, we see that there are no organs or senses to negate at all, just ideas.

Spend as much time as necessary on the senses and their percepts. Return to them every day during meditation or while you have a spare moment at work or school. Intuition, after all, is hard to dismantle.

Investigating the past three stages—body parts, body, and senses—can be especially beneficial for people managing physical pain. Just as with other nondual experiences, when most of us experience pain, we either resist it or fuse with it. Pain then consumes our identity, eclipsing and subsuming our awareness until pain is all that there is.

But Neti-Neti teaches us that we are not our pain, and nor is it "ours." We need not define ourselves by, or even identify with, the pain (nor must we flinch from or resist it, for that matter). The deeper we inquire into its nature, the less solid it becomes. Pain, thoroughly investigated, diffuses and is revealed to arise and subside like the ocean tide. It surges, throbs, and recedes. Pain is not a "thing" any more than anger is; it simply *Is,* because it precedes the labels we attach to it.

In reality, pain is neither good nor bad, for it has no reality as a "thing." Pain is simply another idea or label, as is "good" and "bad."

This realization can be radically liberating, for the less we identify with pain and distress as "mine," the freer we are to experience them without the accompanying layers of mental anguish. We are beyond the idea and sensations of "pain."

There is only Thusness.

Emotions

Select your most powerful emotions and ask, "Am I anger [or fear, or anxiety, or love]? Where is the "I" in these?" Since these are familiar emotions, summon them. Experience them fully, investigating them for their true nature. Move through the entire range of emotions you often experience and consider if they are "I" or even a possession of yours. Of course they aren't. How could they be?

Can anger ask, "Am I anger?", or any question for that matter? Obviously not, because anger has no capacity for intelligence, sentience, or inquiry. They occur within a much larger sphere of experience called awareness or consciousness.

Make sure to address *all* of the emotions that you normally experience. For instance, if you are frequently or easily made sad, then on the deepest, most fundamental level, you need to truly understand that you are not sadness, nor is sadness yours. No trite "I know" will suffice, for when we are consumed with sadness, it feels like sadness *is all that there is*. During these times, everything is tinged with dolor. So it is critical to see through the emotion as a distinct "thing" possessing any ultimate reality whatsoever.

The same applies to so-called positive emotions as well. Joy, happiness, bliss, or elation, while pleasant, are not "I," "me," or mine. Sorry.

We must internalize this truth in the core of our being—we are not any of these. We are beyond them, for "happy" and "bitter" are only labels. What we are, our true nature, transcends all labels.

Take as long as necessary on the emotional stage, in order to fully see through the ones that are the most powerful and thorniest for you, the ones that frighten you the most. Realize that none of them are you or have selfhood, and that what we call "fear" or "envy" is really just a thought accompanied by a specific physical sensation. Emotions have no reality of their own, for like all phenomena, they are just ideas that we superimpose over seamless reality. Once we penetrate into the insubstantiality of "sorrow," we realize that "sorrow" is just a thought. It is not "I," "me," or mine, for we transcend all ideas.

As with physical pain, this dimension of Neti-Neti can be enormously liberating for those suffering from emotional or psychological distress. If, say for instance, we are experiencing an episode of depression or anxiety, we usually identify so much with it that we think we *are* depressed, that we and depression are identical. But this is not the case at all. Emotions and their states cannot limit, let alone define, us. They are passing and fleeting flashes in our experience, while we are completely unconditioned by such ephemera.

Sensations arise from Nothingness, last for a bit, then subside back into Nothingness. We get caught inside of the label "depression" or "anxiety" and freeze the experience into a "thing," when, in terms of manifest reality, there is actually only Thusness— reality void of all labels or concepts.

Roles

Identify your most common social and familial roles. You are not them. This is my favorite stage. Summon a role such as father, mother, sister, friend, artist, teacher, Christian, Buddhist, etc. As the role comes to mind, explore the personal relationships that the role entails. For instance, as an employee, consider your connection to your employers and clients.

What emotions do each of these relationships carry? Experience them. Realize that you are not these roles or relationships, that they are temporary functions we play, not our true nature. Once again, humans have made nouns where none ultimately exist.

You can move through these roles rather quickly, for once you realize that you are not a cousin, then you can understand that you are not a CEO or mechanic.

We are not the things we do. We transcend all of these roles, and thus they can all be seen through as concepts, and thus relinquished.

The same can be said about the objects we own or anything we can "possess." We are none of these. We are beyond them all. They are all Neti-Neti.

Thoughts

In this stage, actively think. Hear your internal voice and ask, *Where do these thoughts come from?* Try to trace them to some point of origin in your mind. Since we ordinarily identify so closely with our thoughts, which probably sound like our own voice speaking in our head, we may need to spend the most time on this stage.

We are not our thoughts. If we were, we would wink in and out of existence with their comings and goings. Thoughts are impermanent; our true nature is beyond time.

Ask: *Where is this "I"? If I am aware before and after thinking occurs, then how can my thoughts be "me"?* Dig into the source and true nature of the thoughts and relentlessly ask, *Where do the thoughts come from? Where do they go?* You'll notice that thoughts suddenly appear from the formless, ungraspable Void of mind. They, like all phenomena, are manifestations of the Absolute.

You are the ineffable, unlocatable Void from where all of reality springs. Or rather, that is all that there is, for in truth there is no "I" at all. In Vedic terms, *Tat tvam asi:* "You are That."

Yet before we can realize that we and all of reality share the same nature as the Absolute, we must detach ourselves from our thoughts in order to see that we are not limited or defined by them. Thoughts, regardless of their content, have absolutely no correlates in the real world. There are no "frogs," "pencils," or "people." There is no "I." These are just ideas, artificial impositions on nondual reality.

Reality precedes and transcends concepts. It is beyond this or that idea.

This particular step is very important because it can be used to bypass the manifest realm entirely—including nonduality—and lead one instantly back to the Absolute. When we look into our minds and try to find the source of our being, to locate the origin of our thoughts, all that we find is emptiness. That emptiness is our true nature. We are that limitless Void of Nothingness.

THE Story

Identify the story you tell about yourself, and destroy it. We all have a central narrative that we tell ourselves about who we are. (Actually, we have many stories, each of which represents a sub-personality of sorts, but for the purposes of the meditation we will tackle one main story or voice.) Our story helps shape our lives and worldview, and frame our experience. *I am the victim, the loner, the rebel, the smart person, the dumb child,* the list goes on and on. Take your pick. We tell ourselves these stories all of the time. But they are just that—stories.

They are no realer than Huckleberry Finn is. Both are complete fabrications. Just like when Mark Twain strung adjectives together to describe Huck, they never landed on him, there is no "I" that we can pin or attach qualities to. Neither Huck nor "we" exist.

Dig into your personal story and realize that you are not that person in the story; he or she is a character. That's right, everything you have ever told yourself about yourself is a story about a fictional character who has your name. You are not that person; no one is. He or she is utter fiction.

How's that for a head trip?

I intentionally do not offer any questions for this stage of the process because no questions are strong enough to topple this fortress. You simply need to take a sledgehammer and obliterate this story about yourself.

It is not you. You were not the cool kid or the dork, the star football player or the shy kid in class. No one was. Those are just stories strung together, draped over a convenient and arbitrary set of linear events, where no subject "I" truly exists. The "I" is the most amazing piece of artifice conceivable.

Notice how you actively maintain this story through your memories, and how this story reinforces your identity and sense of self. This is not coincidental. Our identities are masterfully crafted constructs that rely upon consistency in all dimensions of our being. That means a central, overarching narrative that "brings it all together," as creative writing teachers would call it.

While the language for this stage sounds violent, I use it more for dramatic effect to encourage readers than for accuracy because *there is nothing to demolish.* As with all of the other stages, in reality there is no "I" to negate. Once the "I" is seen through, transcendence comes as naturally as wetness does to water.

The "I Am"

Try to isolate the innate sense of "I Am-ness." I say "try" because the closest we can get to pinpointing the "I Am" is a series of nervous responses, as if, the moment before we've found it, we reflexively flinch as if we were about to fall off a giant cliff into...ourselves. And in a way, we are. We have an instinctive tendency to resist gazing into our own emptiness.

The "I Am" is the subtlest sense that we possess; it is an intuition of our own self-existence, our own being-ness. Often we mistake our volition or will for our "self," but this too is a dead end. For where does the will come from? As we discussed earlier, it arises after-the-fact. It is a result, not a cause.

All of these impressions are completely false, for the simple fact that **anything we can perceive is not us.** The eye cannot see itself; the ear cannot hear itself; and the mind cannot *know* itself. Awareness can never catch hold of its own tail. **Anything we can identify as a percept is an idea.**

This is the most challenging of all the stages to successfully transcend, which is why it's last. Seek this "self" out; see if you can definitively locate it. All you will find, however, is a vague impression of existence, void of a substantial "I." For there is no "I" as an agent or subject with volition. There is simply emptiness, and perhaps a residual, subtle sense of being with no solid reality to it at all.

Nisargadatta taught that the "I am"—our intuitive sense of I-ness or being—is a portal through which we must step in order to know who and what we truly are. The Absolute lies on the other side. We must be willing to shed all vestiges of who we think we are before we cross that threshold. In a sense, we must be willing to die, for no "I" can ever know the Absolute. The latter extinguishes the former.

Ask yourself, *Do I exist?* Of course you do, or at least you think that you do. That visceral, instinctive response is the "I am." Penetrate that completely. Stay with that,

Nisargadatta would say, day and night, and soon that too will dissolve, revealing the great Nothingness behind all of our experiences.

Study that sense of your own beingness as intently as a cat hunting a bird. You are not the "I am." Like everything else we have examined, it is not ultimately real. It is Neti, Neti.

What is the one thing that remains after all else has been negated? What cannot be discarded because it is utterly unmanifest?

It is the Absolute, the Void. That is your true face. Discard everything which is not That.

Chapter 5
Putting It All Together

Now that we have negated, step by step, most or all of the dimensions of what we normally consider constituting the self, "I" or "me," we must put it all together. The previous stages are like warm ups and this is the main event. In a manner of speaking, we are going to flick the switches on our internal circuit breaker, one by one, and when they are all OFF, investigate what remains.

For that is our true nature.

Sit upright once again, find a comfortable position, and close your eyes. Allow your breathing to slow and relax; follow its movement with your mind. Feeling your body, ask:

Am I my body? Don't be satisfied with a rote or robotic response. Dig into the core belief that you are or own your body. If that were the case, where is this "I" *in the body* or *as the body*? Allow the breath to guide and ground you in the physical experience of the body. *Where is this "I"?*

Nowhere. Our true nature is not perceivable or conceivable. It is beyond all ideas, including the arbitrary designation called "body."

Now move on to your senses, emotions, social roles and relationships, thoughts, personal narrative, sense of volition and "I Am-ness." While you shouldn't rush this, the more adept you are at this process, the faster you will move through it. In fact, sometimes the quicker you barrel through the series of inquiries, the more momentum you build.

Is the "I" any of these? If so, where is it? Realize that all you have ever perceived and conceived of are just ideas; thus, you are none of these.

Now declare, with absolute certainty: "**I am NOT my body, NOT my emotions [list some strong ones that have personal significance like depression or anger], NOT** my roles [list them, mother, sister, artist, lawyer, meditator, Buddhist, Christian, noting the emotions or impressions attached to them], NOT my thoughts, NOT my personal story [give details], NOT even the feeling of 'I am.'

"I am none of these."

You can imagine flipping the switches on a mental circuit breaker until they are all off. Allow the certainty and profundity of the realization to resonate and then settle:

"I am none of these."

Let it all drop away, the whole internal and external world, then ask,

"After all of these things have been eliminated, what remains? What am I?"

I won't offer an answer because anything we can put into words is NOT it. Let go of any and all answers and become the answer. Or maybe it might be more helpful to say, *don't* be the answer. *Don't* be anything at all.

That is what you truly are—the complete absence of all predication.

Anything that comes and goes is NOT you. What remains when all of those things disappear? What existed *before* your body was born, before your feelings and thoughts emerged, prior to the emergence of any sense of "I"-ness, prior to even awareness or consciousness? What will exist *after* all of them disappear?

What happens to you—or at least what you think you are—when you die? It's not some heavenly, disembodied consciousness, what is it?

If you were to shed each of these layers one by one, flip the switches on the metaphorical circuit breaker, what would remain when you are all done?

Before the universe—before nonduality, Thusness, the entire manifest realm—what is there?

Where do "you" go during deep, dreamless sleep?

Choose one of these questions and let it fill your entire being like a ball of fire.

What is the ONE thing that has always been, never changes, and will always be present everywhere? Before you were born, before the Big Bang. What is it?

What is prior to you reading this right now? What can never be negated or transcended? What totally precedes "you"?

Words can't touch it, can't express your true face. Zen teachers just pound their teaching sticks on the floor as an answer.

There is only the formless, attribute-less, unconditioned, unmanifest Absolute. The *That-less That* before all else, that is your true nature, your original face before your parents were born.

Chapter 6
Everyday Transcendence

If only life or practice were so cut and dry. I would be lying if I said that the journey ends here. This is only the beginning.

Zen literature abounds with stories of adepts who have had one, two, even three transformative insights into their true nature. These represent radical shifts in self-awareness, and yet these masters spent the rest of their lives developing this understanding, solidifying and digesting it, and ultimately trying to embody it.

In Korean Zen, this is called "sudden Awakening, gradual cultivation." Neti-Neti Meditation is designed both to induce an Awakening experience *and* to offer a practical, complete way of embodying that awakening in this world.

True meditation is being awake to the Absolute moment after moment. I call this "everyday samadhi," or oneness with life. So what if you have a deep spiritual experience, where is it now? Have you resorted to all of your old habits and patterns or are you personifying the certainty of your true nature?

States come and go, so don't try to hold on to them. More important than any fleeting state is understanding that the entire world of form is a manifestation of the Absolute. That is the heart of Neti-Neti.

The paradox of the entire process is that, by the end, after we have returned to the Absolute, we come to embrace all of those very things that we originally negated, for they are all expressions of It.

Some call it the Self, Nirvana, Buddha Nature, Dharmakaya, One Mind, and on and on. The name is not important. Finding it—discovering that THAT is who and what you already are, have been, and always will be—and embodying it is a life practice. This is, I believe, what Socrates meant when he said that, "The unexamined life is not worth living."

Neti-Neti is a continual process, for although I have summarized it in about 16,000 words, in reality its value and import can never be captured or contained, least of all in words. It transcends limitations, for ultimately that is what Neti-Neti negates—the boundaries of form, self, and mind; the limitations of finite being. What continues is simply, "beyond, beyond."

The process never ends, for as Buddhists chant, "Delusions are endless; we vow to cut through them all." The moment we think that we have IT, we have been seduced into thinking there is some final "thing" for some "I" to know. We couldn't be further from the truth.

If we believe that we are enlightened, we aren't. No "I" can enter the Absolute. The "I" is just a provisional label that we assign to the flow of experience interpreted by our nervous system. It serves a social function, but should not be taken too seriously, just like our favorite TV character. Sure, George Costanza is fun to watch, but I don't believe that he is real.

Practice is endless. We must be ever vigilant not to be enthralled by our old habits, labels, and stories. Yet, despite what the Buddhist chant claims, no cutting is necessary—*seeing* is.

Neti-Neti serves as a pair of eyeglasses to cure our myopia regarding the "I" and the entire manifest realm as being ultimately final. We are not our bodies, thoughts, jobs, memories, or anything else that we normally identify with. These impermanent, fluctuating passersby have no reality; they are mere mental superimpositions on nondual reality. They are ideas with no correlates in the real world.

And still, even nondual Suchness is incomplete. Anything that can be perceived or conceived is not the Unconditioned; therefore, mind, form, and consciousness can all be negated. That which *cannot* be discarded is your true nature. In order to realize it, *and maintain that realization*, we must constantly wield the sword of wisdom that is Neti-Neti.

When life offers us a new situation, as it inevitably will, ask, **"What is *this*? Am I *this*? Is this It?"**

Even though we like a neat and tidy "yes"—because ultimately all manifestations are appearances of the Unmanifest—any verbal answer is conceptual.

Zen Master Seung Sahn offered a genius response, "Don't know," an answer that skirts between the duality of "yes" or "no." Reality, both manifest and unmanifest, is unknowable. As William Blake knew very intimately, even what we call a grain of sand is beyond names and conceptual knowing, not to speak of the formless Absolute.

Whatever we encounter is simply Thus, beyond all predication. It escapes and transcends words. As do we. As does everything. What matters is not what we call things, but how we relate to them. Compassion is the hallmark of insight and wisdom.

Neti-Neti severs our attachment to words, revealing their ultimate unreality, and eventually the great Nothingness at the heart of all being. But even that last statement must be seen as provisional, for Neti-Neti does not offer any interpretation, philosophy, or assertion. It negates them all, exposing them all for what they are— concepts—which, of course, we are beyond.

Do not slip back down the muddy path of delusion. You have all that you need. When confronted with a distracting desire or impulse, simply ask, *What is this? Is this "I"? Is this It?* Let that be your guide.

Return to the empty Source that transcends all forms, categories, and concepts. Be THAT, moment after moment after moment.

Chapter 7
Tat Tvam Asi—Thou art That

Neti-Neti Meditation has only one aim: to reveal what you are by negating what you're not. And what aren't you? You aren't anything that you can perceive or conceive of. If you *think* that you truly know something, you don't; all that you "know" is an idea. Whatever you think something is, it isn't.

What Neti-Neti does is uncover the conceptual framework we have superimposed over reality, and then demolish it, leaving only naked, immediate reality. That is nonduality.

Then, by negating the entire manifest realm, we proceed to the Absolute.

We do not live in a world of objects like trees, cars, buildings, and people. None of those have any reality outside of our thinking minds. This doesn't prevent us from interacting in the world one bit. You can still call your grandmother on her birthday (you better) and arrive at work on time. The fact that we live in a world of conceptual currency in no way prohibits or excuses us from wholeheartedly engaging our lives.

In fact, it frees us to do just that.

Once we realize that all notions of separation and discrete individuality are illusory, that everything we have ever come to believe is real is ultimately Not—including all of manifest existence—then we can recognize our true nature beyond all ideas. *Neti-Neti.*

We are That.

And so is everything else, except there is no "I," "you," or "beings" to enjoy it. The vast, seamless whole of reality is an expression of the utterly Unmanifest. That's what we are.

The great Not-That.

Neti-Neti is not an easy process by any means. It takes discipline and courage to confront, negate, and transcend who we think we are. In fact, it requires that we do the unimaginable—relinquish all notions of ourselves and the world as being finally real, and return to who and what we truly are.

We must have the bravery to see past the illusion of selfhood and leap into the empty abyss of impersonal Suchness. This requires more than surrender; it demands self-transcendence.

Then we must be willing to relinquish even that.

In order to win the ultimate prize, we must pay the ultimate price. The entire world of form—all of being and existence—must be negated until there is only the Absolute. Then everything is yours.

Abandon the false self in order to realize the true one. You are "not this, not that"; you are "beyond this, beyond that."

Thou art THAT.

Welcome home.

References

You Are Not: Beyond the Three Veils of Consciousness and *Rays of the Absolute* by Dr. Stephen Wolinsky

I Am That by Sri Nisargadatta Maharaj

About the Author

Andre Doshim Halaw is a Zen Buddhist priest in the Five Mountain Zen Order. He is also the guiding teacher of the Original Mind Zen Sangha in Princeton, NJ. In November 2012, Andre received *inka* (independent teaching authorization) from his teacher, Zen Master Wonji Dharma (Paul Lynch).

Andre writes two blogs. The first, Original Mind, concentrates on Zen Buddhism: www.originalmindzen.blogspot.com. The second, Absolute Nothingness, focuses on Neti-Neti and awakening to the Absolute: www.absolutenothingness.wordpress.com.

He is married, has two young children, and teaches high school English in central New Jersey. He also writes fiction.

Andre offers instruction in the Neti-Neti Meditation process for individuals, groups, meditation clinicians, and wellness/integrative therapy professionals. If you are interested in booking or attending a meditation retreat, instructional seminar, workshop, or simply want more information about Neti-Neti, you can visit Andre at www.netinetimeditation.com.

If you enjoyed this book, please consider leaving a review on Amazon or wherever you purchased it.

Made in United States
North Haven, CT
02 September 2022

23593943R00030